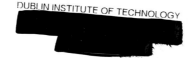

Picasso

WATERCOLOURS & DRAWINGS 1896-1934

Picasso

WATERCOLOURS & DRAWINGS 1896-1934

Contents

Delivering world class engineering design, project management and technical services to our clients in industry, commerce and the public sector in Ireland and overseas.

Irish Examiner

THE IRELAND FUNDS

Peace Culture Charity

Liberté • Égalité • Fraternité
RÉPUBLIQUE FRANÇAISE

THE FRIENDS OF
THE CRAWFORD
MUNICIPAL ART
GALLERY CORK

PUNCH SHOE CARE
Celebrating 150 years
in business

FÁS

C.D.G.A.

ENGINEERING
CONSULTANTS
LIMITED, CORK

Foreword

The new wing at the Crawford Municipal Art Gallery, completed just over a year ago, was built to enable exhibitions of high quality to be presented in Cork. The present exhibition of watercolours and drawings by Pablo Picasso is probably the most important seen in this city for many years, and demonstrates the capabilities of the new wing to provide a service to the people of Cork and visitors to the city.

The sixty-seven drawings and watercolours in this exhibition have been kindly loaned by Musée Picasso in Paris, an institution founded in 1985 as part of an agreement between the French government and the heirs to Pablo Picasso's estate. The collection contains works that the artist retained through his lifetime, considering them to be of significance, marking points of departure or radical changes in style. Spanning the period 1896 to 1934, the works selected for this exhibition all relate to the theme of the human figure, a dominant aspect of Picasso's art throughout his life. They also represent the most important phases of his career.

Although credited with extraordinary powers of innovation and creativity, Picasso was also an artist in the classic mould, developing his concepts through sketches and drawings before embarking on finished paintings. For this reason, the works shown here in Cork, as well as being impressive in themselves, provide a key to understanding the creative imagination of a key artist of the twentieth century.

ACKNOWLEDGEMENTS

The Crawford Municipal Art Gallery is indebted to the Musée Picasso for their support and assistance with this exhibition. Particular thanks are due to Gérard Régnier, director of the museum, Dominique Dupuis-Labbé, curator of graphic art, and Hubert de Boisselier, registrar. Thanks are also due to the Réunion des Musées Nationaux and to the staff of the Picasso Administration for their co-operation and help.

The staff of the Gallery, in particular exhibitions officer Anne Boddaert, have worked hard to make this project a success. The City of Cork Vocational Education Committee administers the Crawford Gallery, and under its chairman Jim Corr, and Gallery board chairman Liam Burke TD, the programming and service to the public has been greatly enhanced since the completion of the new wing. Special thanks to Jamie Monagan, Lucy Dawe Lane, and to Rosalind O'Brien and Chris Byrne of the Friends of the Crawford Gallery.

The Initial Emotion[1]

DOMINIQUE DUPUIS-LABBÉ

Taken as a whole, the drawings of Pablo Picasso shown at the Crawford Municipal Art Gallery exemplify the artist's interest in the representation of the human figure, and are, therefore, testimony of his attachment to reality. One cannot but think, when looking at the faces and bodies Picasso submits to our gaze, about what Henri Matisse said in 1908: 'What interests me most is not still-life or the landscape, it is the [human] figure. It is the figure which best allows me to express the feeling, one might even say religious feeling, that I have for life. I don't care to detail every particular of the face, to render them one by one in their anatomical exactitude. If I have an Italian model, the first sight of whom suggests nothing more than a purely animal existence, I nevertheless discover in him some essential traits. I discern, among the lines of his face, those which best reflect that quality of great seriousness which persists in all human beings.'[2]

The human being was to fascinate Picasso throughout his life, whatever the image he generated, from realism to metamorphosis. It fascinated him to a point where it would become unimaginable for Picasso to conceive of abstract painting, which to him amounted to painting about painting. What could he mean by this? Simply, that painting should not be directed toward the contemplation of itself, nor should it question its own existence through purely formal research into composition, perspective, the rapport between colours, the treatment of space within a painting. The appearance of abstract painting, concurrent with the historic years of Cubism, more than likely troubled Picasso, who showed his feelings on the subject many years later, thereby enlightening us about his own working methods: 'There is no abstract art. There must always be something to start with. One can then remove all appearance of reality from it: there is no danger anymore because the idea of the object has left an ineradicable trace. It is the object which enthused the artist, excited his ideas, put his feelings into motion. Ideas and emotions

Etude pour 'l'Entrevue':
profil de femme au chignon
1901/02 (MP 444)

*La mère et la soeur de
l'artiste brodant*
1896 (MP 409r)

will be forever prisoners of his work; whatever they do, they will never be able to escape the painting; they are an integral part of the work even when their presence is no longer discernible. Whether he likes it or not, the human being is an instrument of Nature, it shapes his character, his appearance.'[3]

Picasso never ceased to scrutinise the appearance of men and women and what that conceals, and it is this he bequeathed to us – endless questions about love, life and death, about the self and about others. These issues imbue Picasso's art with aspects of his personal history, images in which anybody can, in any way they wish, find their own.

Let us perhaps examine a few stepping stones which may lead us to the conclusion that Picasso only recognised the predominance of nature the better to impose his own rules on it. Picasso grew up in an almost exclusively feminine atmosphere. In addition to his mother, Doña Maria Picasso y López (1855–1939), and his sisters Dolorés (1884–1958), called Lola, and Concepción (1887–95), called Conchita, there also lived in the home of his father Don José his maternal grandmother and his father's sisters, Josepha and Matilda. His isolation as the only male in this gynocracy dedicated to education, clothes, and other strictly 'women-only' activities may have contributed to the beginning of his insatiable curiosity about the opposite sex and the feminine mystique, which he adorns in his work with connotations of the erotic. Not so, however, in 1896 when he simply evokes family atmosphere by sketching his mother and his sister doing embroidery, one attentive and skilled and the other awkwardly trying to learn, the tender observation of a young man of fifteen whose immediate surroundings were to be his frame of reference for a few years, and which he would be keen to imprint on paper and to memory. Similarly moving is one of his first self-portraits, brought back by Picasso from his stay, between June 1898 and February 1899, in the little mountain village of Horta de Ebro in the company of his friend Manuel Pallarés. Picasso later confided to a friend: 'All I know, I learnt in the village of Pallarés.' While the remark is probably exaggerated, it seems likely that the artist took great pleasure in the few months spent in the mountains, as shown in the sketches depicting peasants and shepherds in rustic attire. In the sketch *L'artiste dessinant et études de mains*, Picasso, who wears a moustache, portrays himself half-naked and drawing rapidly in a large sketchbook. He is seventeen or eighteen, a powerful moment where we can see the transition from the adolescent to the man, the emergence of the artist, his dark gaze fixed upon us.

Picasso gave his friends from Els Quatre Gats drawings in the same vein – alert, free, and spontaneous. Els Quatre Gats , the famous Barcelona cabaret, was created to imitate Le Chat Noir of Montmartre, and combined entertainment with intellectual life, being frequented by painters, musicians, lampoonists and other rebels. During literary evenings, concerts, or after puppet shows, they spent endless hours comparing their ideas on art and re-inventing the world, as befits every angry generation. These were to be crucial meetings with Catalan artists and intellectuals, often older than him, who were to usher him into an unknown world: the world of culture. Following the example of what was happening in Paris around the same time, with the emergence of Toulouse-Lautrec, Bonnard, Steinlen and Mucha, the commitment of this modernist Catalan group to poster art and printmaking was strong. Competitions among artists experimenting with this new form of expression were frequent. Designed to be put up on a wall, a poster has to catch the attention of passers-by. It must be visually striking, but also it must provide information about the product or the event advertised. On 23 December 1899, the review *Pel y Ploma* (issue 30) announced the opening of a poster competition for the carnival of 1900. The poster Picasso showed at Els Quatre Gats, alongside proposals from other entrants, has disappeared, but preliminary drawings have survived. They show us Pierrot, the extremely popular character from the Commedia dell'Arte, with his powdered face and outsize costume, who becomes the incarnation of the misrule of Carnival.

Projet pour une affiche de carnaval
1899 (MP 427)

Famille de saltimbanques
1905 (MP 500)

Accompanied by a woman, he drinks to the good health of the new-born century. This pierrot presages the moving and vulnerable characters of Picasso's Rose Period – the *saltimbanques* – wandering outsiders who symbolise the reviled artist in the poetry of Théodore de Banville and Charles Baudelaire, as well the paintings of Degas and Rouault.

The *saltimbanques*, or acrobats, with whom he identified through the harlequin character, kept Picasso busy for the whole of 1905. They came into being from the spectacle put on by his Spanish and Catalan knockabout friends of the Médrano circus, located at the foot of the Butte Montmartre. Acrobats, circus riders, jugglers and clowns both moved and amused him. His work becomes a reflection of their everyday lives, of their troubled love affairs, their concerns, their silence and their dreams. The presence of Guillaume Apollinaire beside Picasso/Harlequin, in a china ink drawing of 24 December 1905, is a deeply touching tribute to their friendship and the recognition by the painter of the unsettling perspicacity of the poet, who, a few months earlier, wrote: 'These taciturn Harlequins have their cheeks and foreheads branded by morbid sensitivities. We must not confuse these harlequins with hams. A spectator should be reverent, since they celebrate silent rites with complex agility.'[4]

Emotion, mixed with a keen awareness of love and death, is at its peak in these works, because it is the insecurity and torments of man which Picasso reveals to us. This is painting which is definitely sentimental, but also vibrant and impassioned, as the urge to talk about the self, to observe others, merges with the always greater need to move forward. This necessity explains a barely perceptible shift during the Rose Period, as characters develop from bruised individuals, presented in all their uniqueness, into universal types. Picasso is starting to signify rather than reproduce; the idea of Art is changing. No longer is it simply transcription, and this is confirmed by the more and more incisive attention he pays to resolving figurative problems. From now on, Picasso never ceases to combine feeling and distance, affect and intellect. 'A person, an object or a circle are all figures; their impact on us varies in intensity. Some are closer to our feelings, producing emotions that relate to our desires; others speak more specifically to the intellect. One must accept them all, as my brain needs feelings as much as my senses do. Do you think the fact that this painting represents two people is of any interest to me? These two characters did exist; they don't exist anymore. The sight of them gave me an initial feeling, little by little their true presence became blurred, they became a fiction to me, then they disappeared or rather they have been transformed into all kinds of problems. To me, they are not two people, but forms and colours, but let us be clear, forms and colours which sum up the idea of the two people and retain the vibration of life.'[5]

What Picasso said in 1935 obviously illustrates the Cubist mission: Nature, which Picasso maintains is more powerful than Man, has been domesticated! The painter has taken control; sensibility and feelings take second place because they are dissected and analysed in the name of an art which no longer allows itself to be dominated by appearances. The studies for *Les demoiselles d'Avignon* (1907) or for *Nu debout* (1908) attest to hesitations, changes, and the advances towards the simplification of forms, putting greater emphasis on certain anatomical details, particularly on faces. After Picasso's exposure to African art at the Musée de l'Ethnographie in Paris, he created very basic figures of untamed appearance, deliberately awkward and primitive. These are no longer portraits, but anonymous and impersonal evocations of figures: torsos are dealt with in a perfunctory fashion; shoulder lines and the curve of a breast are signs indicating female figures. Looking at *Nu debout*, we have the image of a tall bather, a reminder of Cézanne, her body simplified in the extreme, particularly the bosom and abdomen, her face only hinted at. Picasso methodically explores the human body: the simultaneous representation from the front, side, back, and/or slightly turned, may come from a need or even an obsession Picasso had for the body. Certainly from the Cubist period onwards the body holds a major place in his work. Cubist bodies, ethereal bodies, bodies monumental from the classical period or monstrous from the 1930s, all underline a desire to possess the body, or sometimes even the very being of the person the artist has in front of him.

It is at the end of the 1920s that the first cruel deformations of the female body appear. Nightmare creatures, castrating women (to whom, from now on, he likens his wife Olga) invade his creative space with their disorder, a space previously dedicated to harmony of line. Picasso frees himself from his chains; he throws his desires and fears onto the canvas. The eruption of Surrealism may have been one of the driving forces behind this return to basic instincts in which love becomes a permanent concern, subjecting bodies to almost unbearable formal contortions. Human bodies are fashioned anew from interlocked spongy or mineral sub-

Etude pour 'Nu debout'
1908 (MP 562)

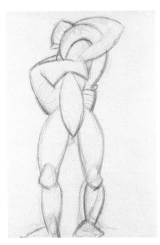

stances in order to form daring erotic metaphors, evoking the essential rawness of sex: 'The powerful and vehement representations of his characters at that time offer staggering metamorphosis. Once again anamorphosis was being talked of ... In fact, it was for him a new organisation of the visible world.'[6]

Christian Zervos, the author of this comment, exactly states the problem. Picasso once again seems to distance himself from reality even while remaining, at heart, rooted in it. He subjects it to all kinds of outrage: the body is under constant re-creation and manipulation, but is nevertheless triumphant. The body, as an enduring link with reality, reminds us that we are not pure intellect, and does so through its basic functions, which must be satisfied, whatsoever they may be. Beyond eroticism even, it is the very materiality of the body, its aptitude for not allowing itself to be forgotten, which probably seduced Picasso. This would explain why he never forgets any of the material details: eyes, ears, nostrils and mouth, even as he associates them with penises and vaginas. The five senses are celebrated to the detriment of the mind. It is the body – the envelope, carnal and strong, sensual and bestial, the site where the two sexes combine – that Picasso favours from now on. The human form anchors him in earthly reality and in the perpetual battleground of desire and its satisfaction.

DOMINIQUE DUPUIS-LABBÉ is curator of graphic art at the Musée Picasso in Paris.

ENDNOTES

[1] The title of this piece was suggested to me by Picasso's conversation with Christian Zervos in 'Conversation avec Picasso', *Cahiers d'art*, special number (1935)

[2] H Matisse, 'Notes d'un peintre' *La Grande Revue*, vol. 52 (25 Dec 1908)

[3] Zervos, op. cit.

[4] Guillaume Apollinaire, 'Les jeunes: Picasso, peintre', *La Plume*, 15 May 1905

[5] Zervos, op. cit.

[6] Christian Zervos, *Picasso: oeuvres de 1926 à 1937* (Editions des Cahiers d'Art, Paris, 1955)

Picasso

WATERCOLOURS & DRAWINGS 1896-1934

Catalogue

PETER MURRAY

◀ *La mère et la soeur de l'artiste brodant /*
The artist's mother and sister embroidering
Barcelona 1896, sepia ink and gouache on paper, 16.5 x 22.2 cm (MP 409r)

Painted in 1896 in Barcelona, this ink and gouache sketch illustrates the remarkable degree of sophistication achieved by the artist, who was then just fifteen years old. Painted most likely in the family's Carrer de la Merce apartment, to which they had moved in the summer of that year, Picasso depicts his mother seated beside his younger sister Lola, whom he often used as a model. While his father José Ruiz taught at La Llotja, Barcelona's art school, where Picasso was a student, his mother Maria struggled to feed and clothe the family on limited means, probably earning extra money by needlecraft. The artist focuses on the heads of the two women, drawing them in fine detail, while their clothing and the room in which they sit are roughly sketched. White gouache is used to create a halo-like effect around their heads. The drawing is a study in contrasts – between the finished heads of the mother and daughter and the agitated marks representing the cloth they are embroidering, and between the contemplative task on which they are engaged and the sense of urgency conveyed in the artist's calligraphy. Ostensibly a picture of domestic bliss, the drawing also reveals an emotional intensity. The artist with his sketchbook forms an invisible third element in this contemplative family group, absorbed in silence in their exacting work.

Scène de corrida / Bullfight scene ▶▶
Malaga or Madrid 1897/98, sepia ink and pencil on paper, 13.2 x 21 cm (MP 425)

From his childhood in Andalusia, through his adolescence in Galicia and Catalonia, and through his years in France, the

Scène de corrida

1897/98 (MP 425)

ritual of the bullfight, the *corrida*, was an important part of Picasso's life and imagination. *Scène de corrida* is a drawing by the youthful artist that captures much of the danger, chaos and violence at the core of the *corrida*. This bullfight scene was possibly done on a visit to Malaga in the south of Spain. The stricken bull – inevitably suggesting a metaphor for Picasso himself – is at the centre of the composition. Matadors advance from left and right, distracting the bull with their capes, while a picador on horseback delivers the final thrust of the lance into the forehead of the weakened animal. Discarded hats and broken lances litter the ground of the arena. The drawing focuses attention on the main protagonists at the moment of death, which becomes an abstract universal truth. There is no attempt to depict the arena or the

crowds. The faces of the bullfighters remain in shadow or are hidden. The lack of specific detail gives the drawing a dream-like quality. This drawing (and others of the period) is inspired by Goya's images of bullfights, with which Picasso would have been familiar.

Projet pour une affiche de carnaval / ▸▸
Design for a carnival poster

Barcelona, end of 1899, oil and black pencil on paper, 48.2 x 32 cm
(MP 427)

As the end of the nineteenth century approached, plans were laid for festivities to mark the dawning of a new century. In Barcelona, the journal *Pel y Ploma* sponsored a competition for the design for a poster advertising a New Year's Eve carnival: 'Carnaval de 1900 Cartell. La Comissio organisadora de les festes del proxim vinent Carnaval, en sessio ordinaria cel-ebrada, als onze dies del corrent, acorda obrir un concurs entre pintors, dibuixants I demes artistes, pera un cartel anunciador de les projecades festes, que tindra lloc segons bes bases que esquiexen.' ('Carnival 1900 poster. The organ-ising committee for the festivities of the approaching carni-val, in their regular meeting, on the eleventh day of this month, have decided to open a competition to painters, draughstmen, and other artists, for a poster advertising the carnival programme, which will take place according to the rules that have been established.') Picasso, back in Barcelona after an unsatisfactory year at the prestigious but staid Madrid art school, did not win the prize, but his design, fea-turing a somewhat pensive pierrot, did attract the attention of Barcelona's artistic élite, among them the magazine's pub-lishers, Modernista painters Miguel Utrillo and Ramón Casas. They promised the eighteen-year-old artist his first exhibition at their artistic café, Els Quatre Gats (The Four Cats). This café, financed by Casas and designed by Pere Romeu, was the centre of the modernista movement and literary and artistic life in Barcelona.

Realising the significance of the opportunity, Picasso made several designs for the carnival poster, at each stage further refining and concentrating his ideas. As with the bull-fight drawing, extraneous detail is eliminated and attention focuses on the central protagonist, who again serves as a metaphor for the artist's own troubled self. Earlier versions of the design show the pierrot accompanied by a woman, both smiling and celebratory, with other figures partying in the background. The pierrot raises his glass of champagne (or cava, the Barcelona equivalent) to greet the new year. However, in this sketch for the final version (which has not survived), Pierrot's companion is masked and his expression is joyless. The figures in the background have disappeared, to be replaced by frenetic and anxious mark-making. The mood of the drawing, done with oil paint and black chalk, has become sombre rather than festive.

▼ Feuille d'études: tête de Christ, vieille femme assise, profil de femme, et main tenant un pinceau /
A page of studies: head of Christ, old woman seated, profile of a woman, and hand holding a pencil
Madrid, early 1901, ink and pastel on paper, 22.3 x 15.4 cm (MP 428)

opposite
Projet pour une affiche de carnaval
1899 (MP 427)

This page of sketches, labelled 'Madrid', dates from early 1901 when Picasso moved to Madrid to collaborate with the Catalan artist Francisco de Asís Soler, on a new art magazine *Arte Joven*.* In the event, not much came of the magazine, but in searching for inspiration for illustrations, Picasso traversed the streets of Madrid and Toledo, sketching people, street scenes, markets and bordellos. The sketches of women have a grotesque quality, but are sympathetic studies rather than caricatures. The faces of the women – probably flower sellers or street traders – are full of character and determination. The head of Christ hints at the strongly religious and devotional character of many of Picasso's paintings and drawings during this period. At the bottom, Picasso has drawn his hand holding a pencil (a sort of clutch pencil for holding sticks of charcoal). Visually, these sketches are accomplished, with strong areas of solid black shadow, highlighted with red chalk.

* John Richardson, A *Life of Picasso*, *volume i*, 1881–1906 (Cape, London, 1991) 177

Femme prostrée au bord d'un lit et tête de femme /
Woman lying on the edge of a bed and head of a woman
Paris, autumn 1901, ink on paper. 25.5 x 37.3 cm (MP 438v)
[not illustrated]

This drawing of a woman half-seated and half-lying on a bed was done in the autumn of 1901. Behind the woman is a crucifix. Picasso in these early years did many sketches and a number of paintings on the theme of the sick bed, probably inspired by the death, in childhood, of his younger sister Conchita.

▶ *Etude pour 'l'Entrevue': profil de femme au chignon /*
Study for 'The Visitation' (or 'The two sisters'): profile of
a woman with a chignon
Paris / Barcelona 1901/02, pencil and frottage on paper, 21.5 x 15.8 cm
(MP 444)

This is a preliminary sketch for the 1902 painting *l'Entrevue*, now in the Hermitage Museum in St Petersburg, which Picasso completed in Barcelona in 1902. In Paris the year before, Picasso had spent much time at the women's prison of Saint-Lazare. Many of the inmates were prostitutes, sent

there 'pour se faire blanchir l'âme' – to cleanse the soul. To set them apart, prisoners afflicted with venereal disease wore a sort of Phrygian bonnet. Picasso himself may have caught venereal disease from visiting brothels at this time.* The prison of Saint-Lazare, run by an order of nuns, was well-known in artistic circles for providing free models, but for Picasso, as for Toulouse Lautrec and Alexandre Steinlen before him, this institution provided authentic subject matter for paintings and drawings of human misery and sadness. The sketches for l'Entrevue show how Picasso, at this time, was creating a hybrid style based on Egyptian, Classical and Gothic art. He was also greatly inspired by the Spanish painter El Greco. The painting l'Entrevue also has another theme. By depicting a whore and a nursing mother together, the artist was probably drawing from the Classical and Renaissance theme of sacred and profane love.

* Richardson, i, 218

◀ Groupe d'hommes / Group of men

Paris or Barcelona, January 1902, pen, sepia ink and pencil on paper,
28 x 19.5 cm (MP 459)

Through the autumn and winter of 1901, Picasso's hopes of achieving success in Paris began to fade and he was forced to ask his father for the train fare home to Barcelona. He returned in January 1902, to a city on the verge of political chaos. A general strike in February was accompanied by street riots, in which ten workers were killed and hundreds more wounded.

This sketch of a group of naked men, heads downcast, may have been inspired by the sight of workers and writers being rounded up and imprisoned in the fortress of Montjuic. Although politically neutral during these years, Picasso's sympathies lay with Barcelona's factory workers, many of whom were recent migrants from rural Spain, fleeing from vineyards devastated by phylloxera. As well as being clearly inspired by the drawings of Théophile Alexandre Steinlen and Käthe Kollwitz (eg Kollwitz's *Cortège de Tisserands* (1897), Collection Neumann), *Groupe d'hommes* reveals the influence of the Catalan artist Ramón Casas, and also of Isidre Nonells, whose paintings of gypsies, vagrants and other marginalised social groups had scandalised bourgeois Barcelona. The sketch dates from the beginning of Picasso's Blue Period. During the following two years, he would concentrate almost exclusively on portraying sad and pathetic people – the displaced poor of Barcelona and Paris, prisoners, prostitutes, *vieillards*, and other social outcasts.

▶ Christ en croix / Christ on the cross

Barcelona 1902, pencil on paper, 37.2 x 26.8 cm (MP 451)

The fervour for anarchism amongst Barcelona's workers was matched amongst the city's middle classes by an equally fervid religious devotion. Some of Picasso's earliest paintings were of religious scenes – paintings of altar boys and first communicants, for which there was a ready market in Catalonia. As the years passed, the young artist's religious sensibility became intertwined with an interest in sex and morbid images of death. This sketch, of a medieval ivory carving of the Crucifixion, was done in 1902. That year saw the founding in Barcelona of the Junta de Museos (Museums Board), set up to purchase works of art for the Museo

Provincial d'Antiguitats, which had been founded two decades earlier, with its wealth of medieval paintings and sculptures. Picasso was inspired by the Catalan Romanesque and Gothic art in this museum. He also made expeditions to remote mountain churches with his friend Joan Vidal Ventosa, who worked on the restoration and photography of the ancient monuments of Catalonia. In this delicate sketch, the dark silhouette of Christ's head, slumped forward in death, contrasts with the slender and beautiful body. This contrast of the sacred and profane is more explicit in a related drawing in the Musée Picasso in Paris, done the following year, which shows the crucified Christ surrounded by naked embracing couples.

▶ Femme implorant le ciel / Woman imploring the heavens

Paris, December 1902, ink on beige paper, 26.1 x 18.7 cm (MP 458)

Prompted in part by the threat of military conscription, Picasso's third trip to Paris was no more successful than the previous two. Penniless and ashamed of his lack of success, he avoided the artists' quarter of Montmartre and his Catalan friends, staying instead on the Left Bank,* and later sharing a room with a sculptor called Agero on the Rue de Seine. In the dim light of their small attic room, Picasso worked on a series of intense drawings, many of them studies for a painting of a deathbed scene he would never complete. Visiting the nearby Louvre, Picasso had been inspired by the tragic theme of Poussin's *The Rape of the Sabines*, from which the figure in this ink sketch may be derived. (It was probably also influenced by the Tahitian paintings of Gauguin.) Successive sketches reveal how Picasso developed the composition. Standing in front of her husband's deathbed, arms upraised, the bereaved woman was to be flanked by her children, seeking vainly to comfort her.

In this ink sketch, the artist has concentrated on the starkness of the woman's grief, a starkness emphasised by the silhouetting of her head and the intense black shadows on her arms and dress.** William Rubin has pointed out how Picasso's graphic style compares with that of Leonardo da Vinci, in that Picasso worked from light to dark, making tones more important than colour. In many paintings, Picasso deliberately lets the tonal underdrawing show through or remain uncovered.

The page is inscribed 'Alfred de Vigny Poésies com-

Alfred de Vigny - Poésies complètes - poèmes antiques
et modernes Les destinées, poèmes philosophiques (œuvre posthume)
Un vol. in-9° edition à st.

plètes – Poèmes antiques et modernes Les destinées, poèmes philosofiques (oeuvre postume) Calmann-Levy edition à 1F' – details almost certainly copied from a book owned by the poet Max Jacob, with whom Picasso stayed in 1902 after leaving the Hotel du Maroc. A devotee of the Tarot, Max Jacob introduced Picasso to mysticism and astrology, which were to become important elements in the artist's work. Jacob also extended assistance to Picasso on several occasions – help which was not reciprocated when, in 1943, the poet was sent to Drancy concentration camp.

* Richardson, i, 253 / ** Richardson, i, 254

Femme nue implorant le ciel / Nude female imploring the heavens
Paris, December 1902, ink on paper, 31 x 23.2 cm (MP 457)
[not illustrated]

This drawing is very similar to MP 458 except that the figure of the woman with her arms raised to the sky is naked instead of clothed in a long dress.

Portrait d'homme barbu / Portrait of a bearded man
Paris or Barcelona 1902–03, pen and ink on paper, 16.8 x 13.2 cm
(MP 453) [not illustrated]

This drawing of a bearded man probably dates from 1902 as it closely compares with the finished Portrait d'homme, a canvas from that year now in the Musée Picasso, Paris. The image of a bearded man appears in many works from this period, symbolising the alienated genius in society, and serving as an alter ego to the artist himself.

▶ Etude pour 'l'Etreinte' / Study for 'The embrace'
Barcelona, early 1903, pencil with scraped highlights on paper,
34.2 x 17.3 cm (MP 474)

The first major painting of Picasso's Blue Period, La Vie (Barcelona 1903, now in Cleveland Museum of Art), is a complex allegorical work that evolved from a series of drawings of a pregnant woman and a man embracing. One of the most powerful of these, Etude pour 'l'Etreinte', shows how Picasso

sought to transform the union of man and woman into a tender and quasi-mystical event suffused with meaning. The subject of the drawing may well derive from an incident in Picasso's own life. In the painting La Vie, the figure of the man originally represented Picasso himself, but the artist later painted in the figure of his friend Carles Casagemas, who committed suicide in 1901.

▼ *Etude pour 'Le couple' / Study for 'The couple'*
Paris 1904, pencil and wash on paper, 37 x 27 cm (MP 481)

In 1904 Picasso returned to Paris, to the ramshackle studios in Montmartre known as the Bateau Lavoir because it supposedly resembled a laundry barge on the river Seine,* where

he would live and work for the next five years. In his journeys to Paris, Picasso was following in the steps of two of Barcelona's wealthiest artists, Santiago Rusiñol and Ramón Casas. Each year of the 1890s they had taken elegant lodgings near the Moulin de la Galette, where they produced academic and polished views of bohemian life in Paris. Picasso could not but hope to match his achievements against the success of Rusiñol and Casas, whose friends in Paris included Miguel Utrillo and Erik Satie. In the Bateau Lavoir, Picasso painted, drew and also produced an etching, *Le repas frugal* (1904), which he hoped would bring him fame. *Le repas frugal* shows two gaunt figures, a man and a woman, seated at a table. In front of them is an empty plate, some bread, two glasses and an empty bottle. The man has his arm around the woman's shoulder; his long, thin fingers give the etching much of its expressive quality. The sketch *Étude pour 'Le couple'* shares many of the characteristics of the etching, save that the woman's hand lies limply on the shoulder of the man, whose face is downcast. It is a study in companionship, and also in shared poverty – two dominant aspects of Picasso's life at this time.

* Richardson, i, 296

Famille de saltimbanques / *Family of saltimbanques* ▶▶
Paris 1905, pencil and crayon on paper, 37.2 x 26.7 cm (MP 500)

In the early years of the twentieth century, families of *saltimbanques*, or strolling circus performers, were a common sight on the streets of Paris. On dusty rugs spread on the pavement, they juggled, performed acrobatics, and survived on the few coins thrown by passers-by. For Picasso, as for the poets Apollinaire and Rilke, these sad harlequin families became emblematic of the artist's peripatetic existence, and of humanity in general. However, in the engravings, drawings and paintings he produced from 1905 onwards, Picasso transformed the street harlequins into quasi-mystical figures, depicting them in diamond-patterned costumes, pointed caps and bells, investing them with the timeless quality of tarot cards. In *Famille de saltimbanques*, the figure of the mother holding her child can be related to drawings Picasso had done some years before in the women's prison of Saint-Lazare. The dog may be Picasso's own dog Feo, while the male *saltimbanque*, like the figures of beggars and outcasts, refers, to some extent, to the artist himself.

Saltimbanque buvant à la cruche / Saltimbanque drinking from a jug

Paris 1905, ink on paper (MP 499) [not illustrated]

This intimate scene, contained within a heart-shaped design, depicts a woman helping a man to raise a jug to his mouth. In nearly all of Picasso's images of *saltimbanques* and harlequins, they are depicted engaged in some simple task, often domestic – holding children, patting a dog, combing their hair, or, in this case, drinking from a jug. The *saltimbanque* and his family became a metaphor for the artist's own search for happiness and domestic contentment, qualities of life not in great supply in the Bateau Lavoir where Picasso lived. However, in spite of the deprivations, Picasso would look back on this period of his life with great fondness, remembering the companionship and generosity of artists and poets who were as penniless as he was. Apollinaire was a frequent visitor to the Bateau Lavoir through the year 1905, when Picasso was working on an ambitious canvas, *Les saltimbanques*, with which he hoped to create a sensation and establish his fame.*

* Richardson, i, 334

Bouffon et acrobates / Clown and acrobats ▸▸

Paris 1905, gouache, ink and wash on grey-blue paper, 23.5 x 15.6 cm (MP 504)

Picasso modelled this figure of a clown or buffoon on an actual circus performer he drew in the Cirque Médrano, identified by the artist as 'El tio Pepe, don José, a 40 ans'. This figure of the buffoon is dressed in the pink tights which were commonly worn by the circus performers of the day. The figure of the seated clown or buffoon appears in different guises in many drawings and paintings done in 1905. Sometimes he is a hurdy-gurdy man, sometimes a satanic-looking monarch. The same figure appears in the final version of the painting *Les saltimbanques*, a sort of father figure of the circus family – a connection reinforced by the similarity of his name to that of the artist's father.* Beside the seated figure, a young girl acrobat dances while another girl acrobat sits on the ground, holding out her hand to a performing dog.

* Richardson, i, 345-49

▾ Portrait-charge de Paul Fort / Portrait of Paul Fort

Paris 1905, ink on paper, 23.5 x 26 cm (MP 1986-42)

The dramatist Paul Fort probably stayed for a period in the
Bateau Lavoir where Picasso lived. Fort employed the artists
of the Bateau Lavoir studios as set painters for his symbolist
productions at the Théâtre de l'Œuvre, just across Place
Ravignan. In March 1905 the first edition of Fort's literary
magazine Vers et Prose was published. The poet André Salmon,
a close friend of Picasso during these years, was literary editor of this magazine, which published new work by writers
such as Gide, Maeterlinck, Apollinaire, Henri de Régnier and
Alfred Jarry.* On Tuesday evenings at the Closerie des Lilas, a
café-restaurant near Montparnasse, writers and artists asso-
ciated with Vers et Prose would meet to drink and discuss art
and literature. At one of these evenings in 1912, Paul Fort was
declared 'Prince des Poètes'.** Other writers who frequented
these Tuesday evenings at the Closerie de Lilas included Jean
Moreas, Maurice Raynal and Henri-Pierre Roche. Raynal was
the financial backer of Vers et Prose, and was not so pleased
with Fort, as the magazine consistently lost money.

In this small, rapid sketch, Picasso has captured the
poet's dashing appearance, his dark hair swept over the forehead, the heavy eyebrows and the waxed moustache that Fort
liked to sport.

* Richardson, i, 296, 319 / ** Richardson, i, 360

opposite
Bouffon et acrobates
1905 (MP 504)

Feuille d'études: arlequins et portraits-charge de Guillaume Apollinaire et d'Henri Delormel /
Page of sketches: harlequins and portraits of Guillaume Apollinaire and of Henri Delormel
Paris, 24 December 1905, ink on paper (MP 509) [not illustrated]

Picasso did many portrait sketches of Apollinaire, but the pear-shaped head of the poet, pipe in mouth, on the lower left of this page of sketches is the closest to caricature. Picasso admired Apollinaire greatly, and so the caricature can be taken in a spirit of fun – more so than the caricature above it of the former horse-dealer Henri Delormel (whose real name was Louis Libaude). As Henry Delormel, he was a well-known literary figure, founder and editor of *l'Art littéraire*, and publisher of Alfred Jarry and others. As Louis Libaude, he was an unscrupulous art dealer, notorious in Montmartre and the Bateau Lavoir for preying on vulnerable impoverished artists, buying their works for a pittance when they were hard-up, and collecting works by artists who were near death, in a macabre attempt to capitalise on their posthumous fame.* The harlequin figure is classic Picasso – androgynous, tender and full of other-worldly atmosphere.

* Richardson, i, 352

◀ *Fernande à la mantille blanche /*   ▶
Fernande wearing a white mantilla
Gosol, 1906, charcoal on paper, 63.1 x 47.4 cm (MP 510)

Several months after moving into the Bateau Lavoir, Picasso met the artist's model Fernande Olivier, who was to become his lover and partner. Fernande's life before she met Picasso had been difficult. An illegitimate child, she had been brought up by a bourgeois aunt who disapproved of Fernande and never let her forget her origins. Trapped in an early unhappy marriage, Fernande rebelled and escaped, finding refuge in the relative freedom of Montmartre, working as an artist's model. In 1906 she and Picasso visited Spain, and after spending several weeks in Barcelona, they decided to travel to Gosol in the Pyrénées, above the valley of Andorra. They reached the village after a long mule ride, Fernande recording her impressions in a journal: 'The village is up in the mountains above the clouds, where the air is incredibly pure, and the villagers – almost all of whom are smugglers –

Fernande à la mantille blanche
1906 (MP 510) |detail|

are friendly, hospitable and unselfish. We have found true happiness here. There is no one here for Pablo to be jealous of, and all his anxieties seem to have vanished, so that nothing casts a shadow on our relationship'.* The couple spent several weeks in Gosol, but when the innkeeper's daughter contracted typhoid, Picasso, who had a morbid fear of illness, decided to return to Paris immediately. This drawing shows how Picasso venerated Fernande, transforming her into a Madonna-like figure, but it also reveals the stifling of his partner's independence which was to lead to their separation in 1912.

* Fernande Olivier, *Loving Picasso: The Private Journal of Fernande Olivier*, Marilyn McCully (ed), (Harry N Abrams, New York, 2001) 183

▲ Etudes pour autoportraits / Studies for self-portraits
Paris, autumn 1906, lead point on paper, 31.5 x 47.5 cm (MP 524r)

Picasso was continually painting and drawing self-portraits, subjecting himself to that same analytical and all-consuming gaze he cast on friends, lovers and models. These sketched self-portraits show the black button eyes, remarked upon by most who knew or met Picasso, which reveal his Spanish ancestry. The pupils are enlarged, perhaps also hinting at the artist's use of hashish and opium during these years. Fernande Olivier's journals record regular drug-taking sessions at the Bateau Lavoir, in which Apolliniare, Paul Fort, Marie Laurencin, André Salmon and other friends indulged. She describes the effect of hashish on Picasso: 'But the effect of the drug on Picasso was more serious. He felt overwhelmed with despair and screamed out that he had discovered photography and might as well kill himself, as he was left with nothing more to learn. He seemed to have had a revelation that one day he would no longer be able to develop. He would reach the end, a well. He would be unable to go any farther. He would no longer be able to learn, or discover, or know, or gradually penetrate the secrets of the art he wanted to transform'.* Although Picasso had indeed acquired a camera, photography aided rather than hindered his development as an artist. The dangers of opium smoking were more real: after an overdose at the Bateau Lavoir, the German artist Karl-Heinz Wiegels hanged himself from a studio window. Picasso, who felt partly responsible for the death of his friend, subsequently gave up drugs. The painting for which these self-portraits are studies is in the Philadelphia Museum of Art. It shows the artist standing, palette in hand, wearing a white shirt, the collar of which seems to have been cut away. In this sheet of sketches, the artist holding the palette is clearly inspired by Velasquez's self-portrait in Las Meniñas, but this reference was not carried through in Picasso's finished self-portrait.**

* Olivier, 215
** Susan Grace Galassi, 'Picasso in the Studio of Velasquez' in Jonathan Brown (ed), Picasso and the Spanish Tradition (Yale University Press, New Haven, 1996) 123

▼ Etude pour 'Les demoiselles d'Avignon': nu debout / Study for 'Les demoiselles d'Avignon': standing nude
Paris, spring 1907, ink on tracing paper, 22.7 x 12.2 cm (MP 537)
[also MP 535, MP 536, not illustrated]

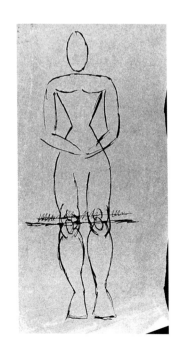

These three studies for what was to become the most important painting of Picasso's career, Les demoiselles d'Avignon, show the care with which the artist approached every aspect of this revolutionary work. The human figure as outlined in these sketches is not based on the canon of human proportions established in western Europe, but rather on a canon to be found in the sculptures of ancient Europe, Iberia, and in sub-Saharan Africa. In this canon, the hips, belly and legs – the centres of human regeneration – are given more emphasis than the head. While Picasso has reduced the head to a simple blank oval, he has treated the knees as if they were the core of the figure's personality. The horizontal divisions in MP 535 show that the legs occupy three-fifths of the figure's height. It was through the intensive study of African sculpture at the Musée de l'Ethnographie (now the Musée de l'Homme) that Picasso was able to bring a monumentality and human vitality to the arid neo-classical canon which had dominated European art through the nineteenth century. The title Les demoiselles d'Avignon may refer to a specific bordello in Barcelona that the teenage Picasso frequented in 1899, when he had a studio at 2 Carrer dels Escudillers Blancs, just off the Ramblas. The bordello was located nearby at 27 Carrer d'Avinyó, today still a seedy area in Barcelona, frequented by prostitutes, drug pushers and tourists.* However, modern interpretations of the work point to a variety of sources, both literary and artistic.

* Richardson, A Life of Picasso, vol ii, 1907–1917 (Cape, London, 1996) 19

Nature morte: poisson, crâne et encrier /
Still life: fish, skull and inkpot
Paris 1908, ink on paper, 47.7 x 63 cm (MP 548) [not illustrated]

The suicide of the artist Karl-Heinz Wiegels in his studio in the Bateau Lavoir on 1 June 1908 had a considerable impact on Picasso, who several years earlier had lost another friend, Carles Casagemas, also through suicide. Just as he had commemorated Casagemas' death through a series of paintings, so now Picasso produced a series of still lifes, including representations of skulls, mirrors and artists' materials, to symbolise, or exorcise, his friend's death.*

* Richardson, ii, 87

▶ *Etude pour 'Nu debout' / Study for 'Standing nude'*
[Paris], early 1908, pencil on paper, 65.3 x 50 cm (MP 562)

In this study, the artist has emphasised the geometric structures that underpinned his evolving view of the human figure. Instead of being rendered in outline or in light and shade – both areas of art in which Picasso excelled – he has challenged his own conventional views by attempting to render the figure almost entirely through intersecting ovoid forms. The pointed oval of the belly is the centre of the figure, as with most African sculpture. The thighs, knees and calves are all roughly ovoid, while the head is barely visible as the upper part of the body is composed of almost completely abstracted interlocking curves.

The painting *Nu debout* (1908), for which this is a study, is in the Museum of Fine Arts in Boston. It is similar in composition to the preparatory drawing, and is painted in vivid blues, earth colours and reds. It is one of Picasso's earliest Cubist compositions. This drawing and other standing nude studies of 1908 can also be related to the painting *Trois femmes* (1908), now in the Hermitage Museum in St Petersburg, and to *l'Offrande* (1908), which celebrates a reconciliation between Picasso and Fernande.*

*Richardson, ii, 80

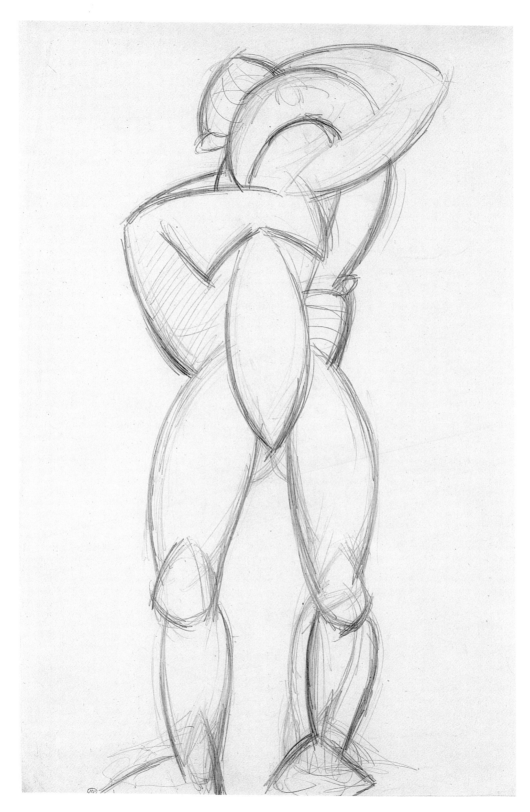

Etude pour 'Nu debout' / Study for 'Standing nude'

Paris 1908, gouache and pencil, 62.6 x 47.8 cm (MP 568) [not illustrated]

This further study for the painting Nu *debout* is close to the final composition in that there is sense of the figure walking forward, while the sweeping lines of the background have been rendered very much as they appear in the final painting. The geometric forms are still evident, but in this sketch the energetic brush strokes of gouache paint dominate the composition. Georges Braque first visited Picasso's studio at the Bateau Lavoir towards the end of 1907 and was astonished at the paintings he saw. Braque himself then began work on a series of paintings of female nudes, paying homage to Picasso.* The relationship between the two artists was complex: Picasso cannily held back from exhibiting his Cubist paintings publicly, allowing the younger French artist to gain the lion's share of publicity at the 1908 Salon des Indépendants, but also of the resulting controversy.

* Richardson, ii, 83

Etude pour 'Nu debout' / Study for 'Standing nude'

Paris 1908, gouache on paper. 64.5 x 45 cm (MP 567) [not illustrated]

In this study, the central figure of the standing nude, composed of geometric ovoid forms, has been filled out with gouache colour, but the background has been left more or less blank.

Etude pour 'Nu debout' / Study for 'Standing nude'

Paris 1908, pencil and violet ink on paper, 32.5 x 25 cm (MP 565) [not illustrated]

While the relationship between this study and the final painting of the standing nude is clear, its relationship to the central figure in Les demoiselles d' Avignon is also apparent, particularly in the woman's left arm, which is bent up and behind her head. Picasso did hundreds of exploratory drawings before embarking on his ambitious painting, which he reworked several times before virtually abandoning it. He drew inspiration from African and Iberian sculpture and contemporary theatre and dance, and also carefully watched the development of his contemporaries, Georges Braque, Henri Matisse and other

Modernist artists. Several drawings and paintings explore the arm-behind-the-head pose, probably inspired by dancers. Picasso almost certainly attended the Richard Strauss–Oscar Wilde opera *Salomé*, first performed in Paris in May 1907.* The dance with veils, the mingling of love and death, and the fear of woman as a destroyer of male virility were things that fascinated the artist, both in terms of venereal disease, which he had probably caught from his visits to bordellos, and in terms of family life, domesticity and the loss of his creative powers. By creating images with the magical powers of African totemic images and fetishes, Picasso hoped to preserve his powers of creativity.

* Richardson, ii, 37

Etude pour 'Nu debout' / Study for 'Standing nude'
Paris 1908, pencil on paper, 32.4 x 25 cm (MP 564) |not illustrated|

In this drawing, the puzzle of what has happened to the woman's right arm is revealed. The arm has been twisted behind her body and she appears to be grasping her side, or her hair, pulling her head downwards. This contorted stance gives the composition strength, but also succeeds in rendering the woman in the image of a slave, held in bondage.

Etude pour 'Nu debout' / Study for 'Standing nude'
Paris 1908, gouache over traces of pencil on paper. 32.6 x 24.9 cm (MP 569) |not illustrated|

In this study, Picasso has framed the figure of the standing nude woman, and has roughly painted in the background as it would appear in the final painting.

◀ Etude pour 'Nu debout' / Study for 'Standing nude'   ▶▶
Paris, early 1908, ink, gouache and wash on paper, 32.4 x 25 cm (MP 570)

The use of ink washes gives this study an energy and vitality that is carried through in the final composition. The figure has been almost entirely deconstructed, to become a series of intersecting curving lines and semi-circular planes. Strong areas of hatching, in ink over violet wash, contrast with areas of brown ink wash.

Etude pour 'Nu debout'
1908 (MP 570)

Etude pour 'Nu debout' / Study for 'Standing nude'

Paris 1908, pen and black ink on paper. 32.6 x 25.1 cm (MP 571)
|not illustrated|

In this study, the figure of the woman is walking forward force-fully, the curving lines of her torso, arms and legs emphasised by strong areas of ink hatching.

◀ Nu assis / Seated nude　　　　　　　　　　　▶▶

Paris, spring 1908, china ink and gouache over traces of charcoal,
62.8 x 48 cm (MP 572)

Inspired by African sculpture, this seated figure of a man is full of a sense of power – the arms folded defensively, a glowering expression, the feet placed apart in an aggressive stance. If this is a self-portrait, it shows Picasso during one of his darker moments of jealousy and anger, of which there were many documented by his partner Fernande Olivier in her journal. She also gave a perceptive description of Picasso's love for African art. 'In the studio, on the table there were African wood carvings, which he had started to collect a few years earlier. I believe that it was Matisse who first realised the artistic value of Negro pieces, followed by Derain, but both of them soon found they had to compete with Picasso, Braque and Vlaminck for the finest examples. Negro art did a great deal for their artistic development. Picasso became fanatical about it and acquired statues, masks and fetishes from all over Africa. The hunt for African works became a real pleasure for him, and he had some pieces that were really appealing in their clumsy way, with their finery, necklaces, bracelets or belts of glass beads.' *

* Olivier, 254

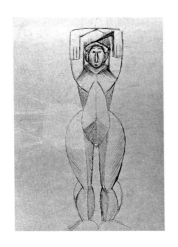

◀ Etude de nu au visage hiératique, les bras croisés au-dessus de la tête /
Study of a nude of hieratic appearance, with arms crossed above the head

Paris / La Rue-des-Bois, summer 1908, ink and sepia ink on paper,
26.7 x 19.6 (MP 551)

In the late summer of 1908, Picasso was recommended by his doctor to take some time in the countryside. Working through the winter of 1907 and the summer of the following year, when the studios at the Bateau Lavoir alternated from freezing cold to baking hot, had taken its toll on the artist's health. The two months, August and September, spent in the countryside at La Rue-des-Bois, Oise, constitute a distinct period in Picasso's work, with nature, in the form of trees and landscape, making a reappearance in his work, along with an emphasis on the use of viridian green in his paintings.

This study of a nude, standing woman resembles the caryatid figures flanking eighteenth and nineteenth-century archways in Paris. However, the artist has deviated from the canon of the classical figure, establishing a new standard based on African sculptures.

◀ *Etude de nu au visage hiératique, les bras croisés au-dessus de la tête /*
Study of a nude of hieratic appearance, with arms crossed above the head
Paris / La Rue-des-Bois, summer 1908, pencil on tracing paper, 31 x 21 cm (MP 552)

This drawing is the same as the drawing MP 551 except that the artist has squared up the sheet of paper in an attempt to systematise the canon of human proportion which Picasso recognised in African art. It is inscribed 'la medita de los dos pantos es el doble de las ancas' ('the measurement of the two parts is twice that of the haunches'). Picasso was fascinated by the visual language for representing the human form which had been developed over centuries by African sculptors. Fernande Olivier relates an anecdote in which a naval officer describes to Picasso how he had met some sculptors in Africa and shown them a photograph of himself. The sculptors, who had not seen photographs before, were unable to see the resemblance between the officer and the photographic image. 'The African laughed incredulously, then took paper and pencil and began to do a portrait of the officer. In his own way he drew the head, the body, the legs and arms in the style of Negro idols and showed the image to the officer. But having looked at him again more carefully, he took back the drawing to add the shiny buttons of his uniform, which he had left out. The point of the story was that he saw no reason to put the buttons in their proper place; they surrounded the whole figure! He did the same with the stripes, which he placed beside the arms and above the head. I don't need to

opposite
Nu assis
1908 (MP 572)

spell out the comments this produced. Afterwards many strange things were seen in Cubist paintings.'* The quiet country hamlet of La Rue-des-Bois, forty kilometres from Paris, proved a little too quiet for Picasso. When his nerves and health had recovered, he and Fernande returned to the city.

* Olivier, 255

▼ Arlequin et sa compagne sur un banc / Harlequin and his companion on a bench
Paris, winter 1908-09, pencil on paper, 22.3 x 27.9 cm (MP 617)

This small sketch contains an extraordinary raw energy, heightened by the artist's rubbing and reworking the outline of the two figures sitting on a bench. Harlequin and his companion are faceless, but they probably represent Picasso and Fernande Olivier. The deliberately awkward rendering of the two figures contrasts with their easy, relaxed attitudes, sitting and conversing. As with so many of Picasso's studies of nude women during this period, Harlequin's companion is depicted with her arm raised above and behind her head. In the spring of 1909 the artist painted a number of works which can be related to this drawing, including La famille d'Arlequin (Von der Heydt-Museum, Wuppertal) and Deux femmes nues (private collection).*

* Richardson, ii, 116

▲ *Femme nue debout / Nude woman standing*
Paris, winter 1908-09, charcoal and pencil on paper, 62.5 x 48.2 cm
(MP 631) [detail]

This sketch can be related to the figure on the left of the
painting *Trois femmes*, begun in the summer of 1908 and
reworked in the months before January 1909, and also to the
extraordinary proto-Cubist *Baigneuse* (early 1909, Museum of
Modern Art, New York). Picasso did not show these revolutionary paintings in the annual salon exhibitions, leaving this
exposure – and the accompanying public ridicule – to the
French artists Georges Braque and André Derain. Instead, the
Spanish artist preferred to have his work seen in the more
sympathetic context of influential collections of avant-garde

art, such as that assembled by the wealthy Americans, Leo and Gertrude Stein. Although Leo Stein had been shocked by the savagery of Les demoiselles, he and Gertrude later acquired Trois femmes, the painting which was to establish Picasso in the public eye as the inventor of Cubism.

In this sketch, the artist again has depicted the woman in a contorted and uncomfortable position, her right arm behind her head, and her left leg raised slightly. In the final painting (now in the Hermitage Museum, St Petersburg) the woman is shown kneeling.* These depictions of standing and kneeling women were also referred to as 'dryads', as if they were creatures of the forest. In their primal, mythic character, they prefigure Igor Stravinsky's The Rite of Spring, performed in Paris in 1913. Stravinsky, who was a year younger than Picasso, achieved fame with the music he composed for the Ballets Russes de Serge Diaghilev in Paris – The Firebird (1910), Petrushka (1911) and The Rite of Spring.

* William Rubin and Dominique Bozo, Pablo Picasso: A Retrospective (MoMA, New York, 1980) 115

Nu assis / Seated nude
Paris, winter 1908–09, black crayon on paper, 32.3 x 21.6 cm (MP 630)
[not illustrated]

In this study, Picasso has reverted somewhat to a sinewy neo-classical image of the female form, and has moved away from the aggressive ovoid forms and geometric planes of the Cubist nude studies. John Richardson points out that even during the most intense years of Cubist experimentation, Picasso would occasionally revert to a more traditional form of representation – as if continually testing the skills he had learnt at art school – before launching himself again into the unknown.

▶ Etude pour 'Tête de femme (Fernande)' / Study for 'Head of a woman (Fernande)'
Horta de Ebro, summer 1909, pencil on paper, 62.8 x 48 cm (MP 642)

In the summer of 1909, Picasso and Fernande again visited Barcelona to see his parents, before moving on to the mountain village of Horta de Ebro (now called Horta de St Juan), where they were to spend the summer months. Picasso had

stayed at this village twelve years before with his art school friend from Barcelona, Pallarès. His visit then had been productive, and he returned to Horta with the intention of concentrating on his art to the exclusion of outside distractions. In Horta, the harsh rocky landscape of Santa Bárbara and stone houses of the village lent themselves to Picasso's development of Analytical Cubism, with his inverted perspective, fragmentary geometric forms, and progressively flattened picture plane. He also painted and drew several Cubist studies of Fernande's head. In some of these studies, Fernande's head seems almost to blend into the mountainous landscape of Horta. When they returned to Paris in September, Picasso sculpted a Cubist bronze head of Fernande (Museum of Modern Art, New York). The bronze head, with its elaborate coiffure, combines Cubist planes with African forms. This pencil sketch is a preparatory drawing for the sculpture.

▸ *Etude pour 'Tête de femme (Fernande)'* /
Study for 'Head of a woman (Fernande)'

Horta de Ebro, summer 1909, pencil on paper, 63.2 x 48 (MP 641)

In this somewhat intimidating portrait of Fernande, her fea-
tures have been entirely subsumed within the geometric
forms of Picasso's Cubist vision. In a letter to Gertrude Stein,
written in July 1909, Fernande records how miserable she was
for much of this trip. She was ill with a kidney infection, and
had to spend most of her time in bed. Picasso reacted with
his usual horror of illness of any kind. 'Pablo is no help. He
doesn't know what's going on and he's too selfish to want to
understand that I'm the one now who needs him.' * After several weeks, Fernande recovered her health. On arriving back
in Paris, Picasso, who was for the first time now making some
money selling paintings, decided to move from the Bateau
Lavoir to a studio and apartment at 11 Boulevard de Clichy,
near the Place Pigalle. The Steins bought two of his Cubist
Horta landscapes, and, according to Fernande, Braque was so
inspired by these that he immediately began to move away
from Impressionism and to adopt the new style pioneered by
Picasso.** This partisan account, echoed in Gertrude Stein's
Autobiography of Alice B. Toklas, is firmly rejected by John
Richardson, who points out that in his paintings of l'Estaque,
Braque had led the way towards Cubism a year before Picasso
went to Horta.

* Olivier, 243 / ** Olivier, 259

◀ *L'homme à la moustache et à la tenora* /
Moustachioed man with a tenora   ▶▶

Paris or Céret, autumn 1911, pen, ink and pencil on paper,
30.8 x 19.5 cm (MP 659)

In March 1911, Picasso had an exhibition of eighty-three
watercolours and drawings at the 291 Gallery in New York,
which consolidated the fame he was achieving on both sides
of the Atlantic. In May he was represented in the Berlin
Sezession exhibition, along with Braque. In early July, Picasso
went to Céret in the south of France, where he was joined
some weeks later by Fernande, Max Jacob and Georges Braque.
Picasso and Braque worked closely together, developing further the Cubist style they had pioneered. In particular, their
sojourn in Céret saw the introduction of text, both calli-

50

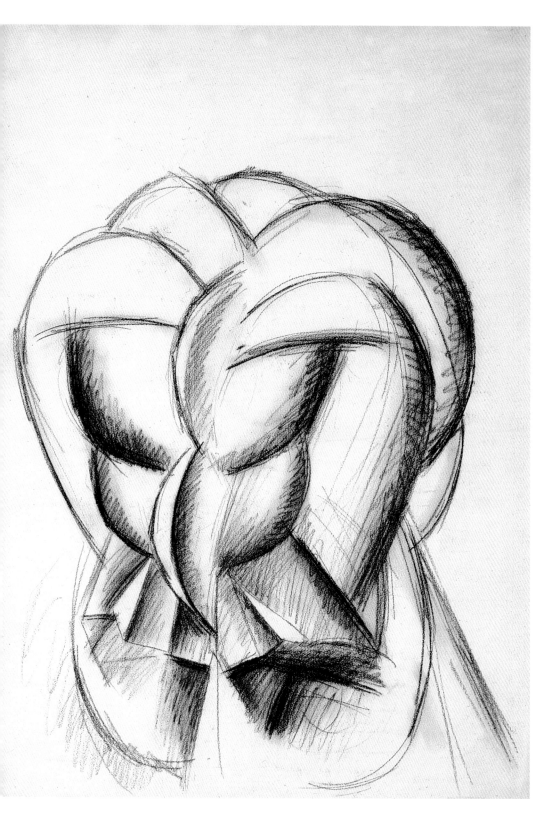

graphic and stencilled, into their paintings.* Using lettering further emphasised the degree to which they had moved away from representational painting towards an art in which conceptual and symbolic qualities predominated. This drawing, almost certainly done in Céret, does not include text, but is nevertheless a classic Cubist composition. The drawing is restrained in colour, a characteristic of Picasso's and Braque's Cubist works from this period. The composition is strongly formalised and carefully balanced on either side of a central vertical axis.

In Céret, Picasso was friendly with Déodat de Séverac, a composer who based his compositions on Catalan *sardana* dance music, and who employed traditional Catalan instruments such as the tenora, a type of double-reeded clarinet. The tenora player formed part of a *cobla*, or brass band, perched high on a wooden bandstand, that accompanies the *sardana* dance. Séverac described the music of these traditional instruments in terms of their colour – the tenora was 'red, red-sunlight'.**

In the autumn of 1911, Picasso's relationship with Fernande began to fall apart, and he met and started an affair with Eva Gouel (Marcelle Humbert), the partner of a Polish artist named Louis Markus. The fact that Eva was also a friend of Fernande did not prevent her from colluding with Picasso in engineering a situation that made it easy for her new lover to break with Fernande. However, Picasso and Eva's years together were few; in 1915 she died of cancer. Fernande was to outlive her by half a century.

* Rubin and Bozo, 122

** Richardson, ii, 189; Robert Rosenblum, 'The Spanishness of Picasso's Still Lifes' in Jonathan Brown (ed), *Picasso and the Spanish Tradition* (Yale University Press, New Haven, 1995) 79

Etude pour 'Femme en chemise dans un fauteuil' /
Study for 'Woman in a shift in an armchair'
Paris, Autumn 1913, black and brown crayon and wash on paper, 18.5 x 14.6 cm (MP 766) [not illustrated]

In 1913 Picasso had his first large retrospective, at the Galerie Tannhauser in Munich. His friendship with Apollinaire continued, his Cubist portrait of the poet featuring on the cover of the volume *Alcools*, published that year, while Apollinaire wrote an essay describing how Picasso had moved from an art

opposite
L'homme à la moustache
et à la tenora
1911 (MP 659)

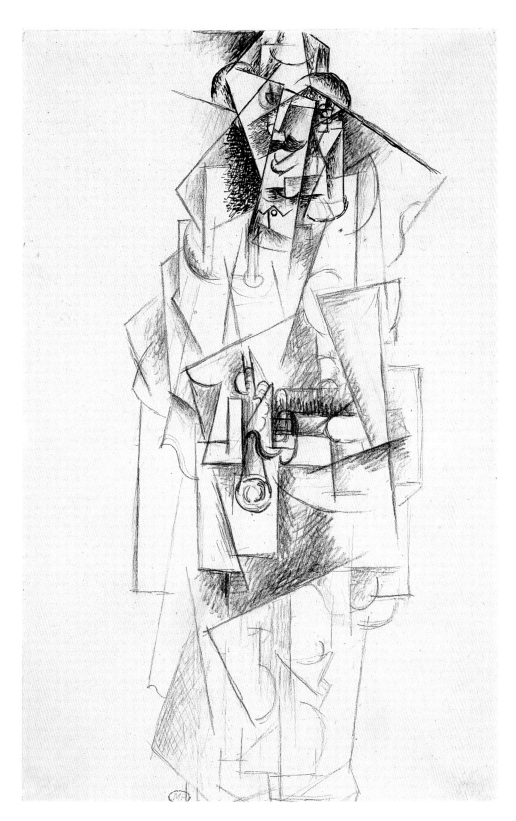

based on representation to one based on conception. In the Armory Show in New York, Picasso was represented by eight works. That year, also, his father died, and the artist went to Barcelona for the funeral, returning to Céret with his new partner Eva, where he completed L'*homme à la guitare*. Picasso and Eva returned to Paris in the autumn of 1913 to a magnificent new apartment and studio in Montmartre, at 5 bis rue Schoelcher.

After seeing Matisse's recently completed, iconic *Portrait of Madame Matisse*, Picasso responded with a Synthetic Cubist portrait of Eva sitting in an armchair (now in the Ganz collection in New York), for which this is a preparatory sketch.* The drawing, coloured with gouache, shows the basic elements of the composition, the figure of Eva signified by simple curves. Her small head, painted like an Egyptian tomb mask, is perched on top of a body composed of large geometric intersecting planes, all contained within the enfolding embrace of the armchair. Disembodied breasts suggest an unresolved sexual aspect, and, perhaps, a degree of hostility mixed with desire on the part of the artist. The drawing contains more detail of the room and floor than appears in the final painting. In this study, as in the final painting, elements of Analytical Cubism combine with the newer Synthetic Cubism.

* Richardson, ii, 288

▶ *Etude pour 'Femme en chemise dans un fauteuil' /*
Study for 'Woman in a shift in an armchair'
Paris, autumn 1913, pencil and gouache on paper, 32.7 x 27 cm (MP 767)

In this highly developed study for the painting, the artist depicts the armchair in a relatively conventional manner, as well as the paneled wall behind. The figure of the woman has a monumental quality, emphasised by the diminutive head surmounting the large, bold, curving planes used to suggest the body. The stylised waves of hair appear in the final painting, but not the woman's face, which bears a pensive expression.

Homme attablé / Man at table
Avignon, summer 1914, pencil on paper, 31 x 23.7 cm (MP 745)
[not illustrated]

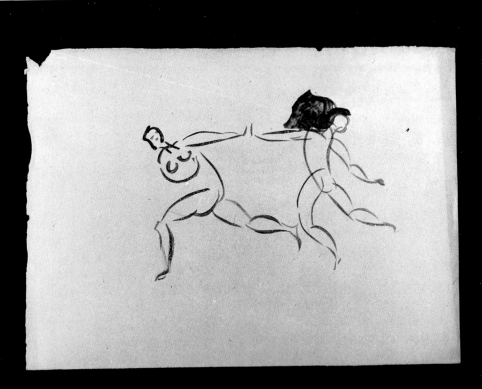

(MP 847)

(MP 848) (MP 849)

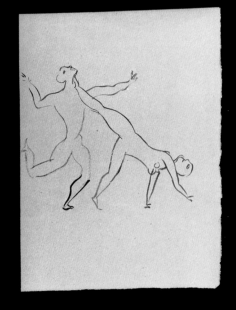

In August 1914, war was declared and Picasso's relatively settled world was disrupted. Braque and Derain were mobilised into the French army, and Picasso, a Spanish citizen and therefore exempt from military service, saw them off at the station. Picasso's dealer Kahnweiler, a German citizen, remained in Switzerland for the duration of the war, but his gallery in Paris, including works by Picasso and Braque, was sequestered by the French authorities. Remaining in Avignon, Picasso continued to work on a series of drawings of men leaning on balustrades, tables and chairs, in styles ranging from naturalism to Cubism.

This drawing is one of those done in a naturalistic style. Returning to Paris, Picasso found a sombre city where he was treated with some suspicion. A further shadow was cast over his life the following year when his partner Eva died after a period of illness.* The drawing of a man seated at a table has a simple, classical feel. Rendered in outline, without shading, it looks back to the social outcasts Picasso depicted at the turn of the century, and also forward towards his post-war neo-classical style. The elongation of the torso is reminiscent of Cézanne's card players, which, like his views of Mont Ste Victoire, were painted not far from Avignon.

* Rubin and Bozo, 178

◀ *Couple de danseurs / Two dancers*
1917, watercolour on paper, 19.7 x 27.3 cm (MP 847)
1917, watercolour on paper, 19.8 x 27.4 cm (MP 848)
1917, watercolour on paper, 26.5 x 19.5 cm (MP 849)

In May 1916, Jean Cocteau brought Serge Diaghilev to meet Picasso and to discuss plans for Cocteau's ballet, *Parade*. Picasso eventually agreed to design the décor for this ballet, the theme of which was familiar to him: a conjurer, an acrobat and a girl performing their acts on the street. In Rome the following year, where the ballet was being rehearsed, Picasso spent time with Diaghilev, Léonide Massine, Cocteau, Igor Stravinsky and Leon Bakst. He also met a ballerina named Olga Koklova, whom he was to marry. After the inaugural performance in Paris in May, Picasso, infatuated with Olga, followed the Ballets Russes to Madrid and then to Barcelona. When the troupe departed for South America, Olga remained behind with Picasso.

As a result of his encounters with the Ballets Russes

and Olga, Picasso now began to mingle with high society. These sketches can be read as lively and humorous episodes from the artist's pursuit and capture of Olga. In the first, a male figure in a Minotaur mask pursues a woman; in the second the man holds the woman aloft; in the third there is a spirited kick delivered by the woman to her pursuer's chin.

▶ *Portrait d'André Derain / Portrait of André Derain*

London, May-July 1919, pencil on paper, 39.9 x 30.8 cm (MP 838)

André Louis Derain came to prominence in 1905 when he, together with Henri Matisse, Maurice de Vlaminck and others, exhibited at the Salon d'Automne. Their paintings, characterised by vivid unmixed colours and expressionist paintwork, earned them the title Les Fauves, or the Wild Beasts. By the end of 1907, under the influence of Picasso and Braque, Derain had abandoned Fauvism and turned to Cézanne for inspiration. However, he never fully adopted Cubism, and by 1918 had repudiated both it and the new abstract art in favour of a more traditional approach. From the 1920s on, a strong classical influence is evident in Derain's paintings and drawings and in the stage designs he produced for the Ballets Russes de Serge Diaghilev and other companies.

This powerful outline drawing of the painter André Derain can be compared to other drawings of Picasso's friends and society acquaintances done this year, including Serge Diaghilev and Alfred Seligsberg. In their pure style of realism, these works display Picasso's prowess as a draughtsman, but when compared with the decorative works he was producing for ballets during this period, and with paintings in the by now well-established Cubist style, it seems clear that a degree of artistic uncertainty and loss of sense of direction occurred at the same time as his encounters with high society in London, Biarritz and other social centres.

◀ *Danse / Dance*

Paris, 18 November 1919, pencil on paper, 16.4 x 11.2 cm (MP 867)

Amongst the paintings and drawings produced during this period, there are some where a sense of sentimentality, which had not been seen in Picasso's work since his early years, returns. This drawing of a couple dancing retains a dignity and sensitive quality without becoming sentimental. The

couple probably represents Picasso himself with his wife Olga, who had given up her career with the Ballets Russes to marry the artist.

Etudes de costumes de 'Pulcinella' et de personnages féminins / Study of 'Pucinella' costumes and of female figures
1920, pencil on paper, 24 x 33.9 cm (MP 1793) [not illustrated]

Picasso, entranced by the world of the theatre into which he was drawn by his wife Olga, produced sketches and designs for several theatre and ballet productions, such as Le tricorne, a production by the Ballets Russes, which was presented in July 1919 at the Alhambra Theatre in London. In December of that year he was asked by Diaghilev to collaborate on Pulcinella, a new ballet on the theme of Commedia dell'Arte, set to music by Stravinsky. Picasso's first sketches for the décor were rejected by Diaghilev as being too modern. Picasso later modified his designs to make them more acceptable to the Russian impresario. The first performance of Pulcinella took place at the Paris Opéra, with décor and costumes by Picasso, choreography by Massine, and music by Stravinsky. Pulcinella, a leading character in the Commedia dell'Arte, is depicted by the artist as a hook-nosed circus ringmaster, watching imperiously while the female dancers pirouette and curtsy. The face of the dancer on the left has been reduced to a simple oval shape, prefiguring the Surrealist method of using artists' lay models and mannequins to represent human beings.

▶ Etude de costume: le mage / Costume study: the magician
Paris c.1920, lead point and gouache on paper, 16.2 x 10.5 cm (MP 1803)

This delightful small sketch was probably done by Picasso as a costume design for a production by the Ballets Russes. In a playful way, also, it encapsulates much of the artist's own reverence for the world of magic and the supernatural. Picasso, very much an artist of the twentieth century, was also noted for preserving superstitions going back to ancient times. For instance, he jealously guarded his nail and hair clippings lest they fall into the hands of someone who wanted to put a curse on him. This was not an idle fancy: after he abandoned Fernande Olivier and took up with his new partner Eva, Fernande claimed later to have cursed him for this rejection.

Fernande also claimed that the premature death of Eva was a result of this curse.*

* John Richardson, 'The End of the Story', *Loving Picasso: The Private Journal of Fernande Olivier* (Harry N Abrams, New York, 2001), 283

▼ *Olga au chapeau à plumes* / *Olga wearing a feathered hat*
Paris 1920, charcoal and lead point on paper, 61 x 55 cm (MP 902)

Picasso and Olga Koklova, a dancer with the Ballets Russes, were married at the Russian Orthodox church in Paris in July 1918, in a ceremony attended by Cocteau, Max Jacob and Apollinaire. The couple spent their honeymoon in Biarritz, staying at the home of Mme Errazuriz. During his stay in Biarritz, Picasso met art dealers such as Paul Rosenberg and Georges Wildenstein. The couple returned to Paris in October. Shortly afterwards Apollinaire died of influenza. With art critics during this period regularly commenting on the passing of Cubism, Picasso's paintings betray a bewildering variety of

styles, from the academic realism of *Olga à la mantille*, through the stylised mannerism of *Baigneurs*, painted in Biarritz in 1918, to the theatricality of his costume and décor designs for the Ballets Russes. His Cubist compositions from this period are accomplished, but have lost some of the hard edge of ten years before. This drawing of his wife Olga, dressed fashionably and expensively, hints, in its emptiness, at Picasso's inner rejection of the world of high society in which he now moved. Their marriage did not survive long. The bourgeois comforts sought by Olga proved increasingly claustrophobic to the artist, who, throughout his life, could never reconcile his quest for an austere and simple existence with his contradictory quest for fame and fortune.

▲ Trois *baigneurs* / *Three bathers*

Juan-les-Pins, 19 September 1920, gouache on paper, 21.2 x 27.5 cm (MP 940)

The irresolution evident in Picasso's work during these years comes through strongly in this drawing of bathers, done in the fashionable resort of Juan-les-Pins in September 1920. Picasso dallied with different styles during this period; there are other similar drawings of bathers, done during the same weeks, in the collection of the Musée Picasso, Paris. Each might well have been done by a different artist. Each, in its own way, points to styles of figuration that were to be endlessly copied by artists through the mid-twentieth century.

▼ Etudes pour 'Trois femmes à la fontaine' /
Studies for 'Three women at the spring'
Fontainebleau, summer 1921, charcoal and red chalk on paper
32.1 x 24.5 cm (MP 966), 24.5 x 32.1 (MP 967), (MP 968)

In the summer of 1921, Picasso, Olga and their baby son
Paulo, born on 4 February, moved to a villa at Fontainbleau.
Among the works produced during this productive summer
was the monumental neo-classical painting *Trois femmes à la
fontaine*, now in the Museum of Modern Art, New York. In this
painting, the three dark-haired women, similar in appearance
and dressed in simple classical gowns, form a group around
a spring of water. The woman on the left stands. From her
forefinger is suspended a terracotta jug. The woman on the
right sits on a rock, her right arm extended. She also has the
lug of a terracotta pitcher held in her forefinger. The right
hand of the third woman rests on her lap.

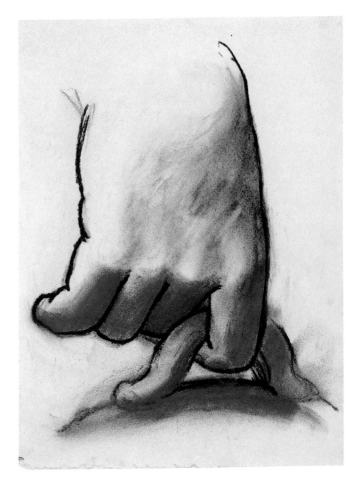

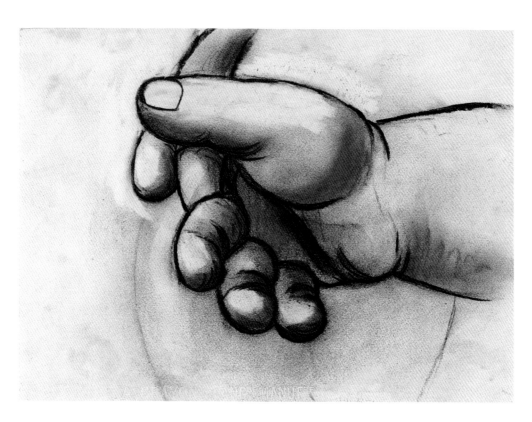

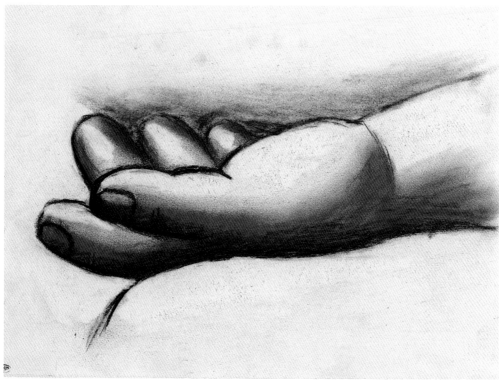

These charcoal sketches for these three hands show how Picasso simplified the painting, giving it a monumental feel. The women's arms and heads seem also to be sculpted in terracotta. By returning to classical themes and styles, Picasso regained a sense of the eternal, the otherworldly, that had characterised his work from the Blue Period and the earlier phases of Cubism.

▼ Olga et Paulo / Olga and Paulo
1922/23, pencil on paper, 11.5 x 8.4 cm (MP 1007)

This pencil sketch can be dated by guessing at the age of Picasso's son – perhaps two years old – who is standing on his mother Olga's knee, holding her tenderly around the neck.

Olga is sitting in an armchair, dressed in a long nightgown. The drawing is light and free, with fluid, swift lines. It depicts a relaxed and loving family scene, yet there is something of a sense of terror in the eyes of Olga, with her young son holding her around the neck as if to comfort her. Outside the room, through the window, an iron balcony is visible, with trees beyond. They are indicated only with the slightest of lines.

◀ *Bal (projet pour un rideau pour un bal de Mardi Gras chez le Comte Etienne de Beaumont)* /
Ball (design for curtains for a Mardi Gras ball at the house of Count Etienne de Beaumont)
Paris, 1923, ink and pencil on paper, 22.4 x 17.5 cm (MP 1553)

This is a simple linear design, with two figures drawn in a humourous Cubist style. The figure on the left, with tritons for feet, holds a fish. The sun-figure on the right holds a staff, on top of which are the letters BAL.

In the summer of 1923 Picasso and his family returned to the Riviera, to stay at Cap d'Antibes. Among the artists living nearby was the American painter Gerald Murphy and his wife Sara, a couple who were to inspire Scott Fitzgerald's novel *Tender is the Night*. Picasso was friendly with the Murphys, and did several drawings of Mrs Murphy. Also staying at Cap d'Antibes was Count Étienne de Beaumont. The following year, de Beaumont hosted a Mardi Gras ball at his house in Paris on the occasion of the first performance of *Mercure*, at which Man Ray photographed Picasso, dressed as a Spanish matador.

Femme dans un fauteuil / Woman in an armchair
Paris, 29 January 1929, pencil on paper, 27.8 x 20.8 cm (MP 1031)
[not illustrated]

In this zany, slightly crazy composition, Picasso has represented a woman sitting in an armchair which has a striped cover. A big foot appears from underneath a dress, while the woman's head is skewed sideways, so much so that her eyes are one above the other. If this is a representation of the new love in Picasso's life at this time, Marie-Thérèse Walter, it hints at a somewhat hapless victim of the artist's mastery of manipulation of people to his own ends.

▶ *Le peintre et son modèle devant le tableau /*
The painter and his model in front of the painting
Boisgeloup, 31 October 1930, ink on paper, 23.1 x 28.8 cm (MP 1049)

This drawing shows Picasso's growing interest during the 1930s in the iconography of the artist's studio and in the revival of Classicism in art that was infused with feeling and emotion. On the left of the drawing the model is posed standing, her left hand raised to the side of her face. On the right, the artist – an Apelles-like bearded man – is painting her portrait. The portrait, in which the woman's head is turned to the right, does not correspond with the pose of the model, whose head is turned to the left. In 1917, Picasso had visited Naples and Pompeii, an encounter with the art of Roman times that left a lasting mark on his work. The work also probably reflects the rekindling of his love life after meeting Marie-Thérèse Walter in 1927. Around these years, the theme of the artist's studio predominated in Picasso's work, from the 1928 *Le peintre et son modèle* in the Museum of Modern Art in New York, to the classically inspired *L'atelier du sculpteur*, a group of forty-six etchings which form part of the *La suite Vollard*. In these paintings, drawings and prints, the artist is both viewer and lover of the model, who has a controlling rather than a subservient role. The idyllic and untroubled scene depicted here can be contrasted sharply with the emotional chaos of Picasso's life during this period.

▶ *Le peintre et son modèle / The painter and his model*
Boisgeloup, 9 November 1930, ink on paper, 12.1 x 18.5 cm (MP 1048)

The painter sits on the right, the model reclines on the a bed on the left. The composition is divided vertically in the centre by the painting panel of the artist, which is supported on a simple tripod easel. The painter's right hand is raised, his brush poised to make a mark on the panel. The classical feel of this work is emphasised by the draperies on the bed, in the background, and on the seat on which the artist is seated. The work with which the artist is engaged is invisible. The relationship of artist and model, the theme of Balzac's *Le chef d'œuvre inconnu* (1831), fascinated Picasso throughout his life. In Balzac's novella, a fictional painter tantalises his friends by telling them of a portrait of a beautiful nude woman he has created in secret. However, when the friends are finally allowed to see the painting, they are shocked at how it differs

from their expectations. In 1927, Picasso had etched an illustration for Balzac's novel.

▲ *Le sculpteur et son modèle / The sculptor and his model*
Boisgeloup, 2 August 1931, ink on paper, 25.6 x 32.6 cm (MP 1051)

A standing nude on the left, a sculptor at work on the right. The female nude is rendered in swirling ink lines. Behind, a dark shape suggests a figure embracing her. The sculptor gazes at the woman and this mystery lover adoringly, his hands under his chin, holding a walking cane. Between the sculptor and the model Picasso has interposed a large hand, completely out of scale, holding a vertical line, as if pulling back a curtain. This hints at the voyeuristic pleasure the sculptor is taking in watching the woman and her lover.

Une anatomie: trois femmes /   ▶▶
An anatomy study: three women
Paris, 27 February 1933, pencil on paper, 20 x 27.1 cm (MP 1094)

At the beginning of the 1930s, Picasso produced two paintings, Le baiser and La baigneuse assise, both of which set out to subvert the notion of the ideal as expressed in neo-classical art. His experimentation also led him to create works clearly within the Surrealist canon. Roland Penrose compares these pencil drawing to the Surrealist assemblages of Alberto Giacometti. Penrose comments on the attacks on Picasso by followers of the neo-classical sculptor Aristide Maillol, particularly Waldemar George, who protested that, 'The Chimeras of Pablo Picasso are destined to be dumb still-lives, assemblages of form and colour, but not sources of energy or foci of a Mediterranean civilization.' * However, in spite of their bizarre and conventionalised Surrealist appearance, these drawings owe a great deal to the neo-classical tradition of single, austere, monochrome standing figures, popularised in France by Maillol. Picasso's anatomy drawings were reproduced in the Surrealist periodical Minotaure 1 in 1933.

* Roland Penrose, Picasso (Phaidon, London, 1991) 98

Une anatomie: femme assise /   ▸▸
An anatomy study: seated woman
Paris, 28 February 1933, pencil on paper, 20 x 27 cm (MP 1089)

In the mid-1920s, the Surrealist movement, led by André Breton, presented Picasso with an ideal opportunity of moving forward from the impasse he had reached with his art. The emphasis placed by the Surrealists on the unconscious, on erotica and the psycho-sexual tied in perfectly with Picasso's reliance on what he regarded as a sacrosanct inner creative impulse that must be defended against theorising at all costs. In retrospect, many of the tenets of the Surrealists appear now as shallow, adolescent and self-serving. However, their work should be viewed in the light of their attempt to break apart the pictorial conventions which had dominated European art for five centuries. Picasso has used the conventions of style established by the Surrealists to express once more his reverence for and fear of women.

This drawing depicts a seated woman, her gender indicated by a vaginal gash, her breasts reduced to a pair of ovals on stilts. In its cartoonish quality, this work reveals the insecurity and fear felt by Picasso whenever he was confronted with female sexuality.

(MP 1094)

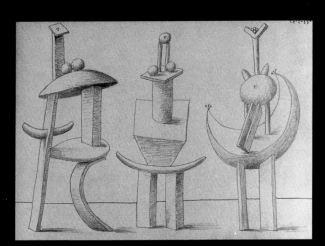

(MP 1089)

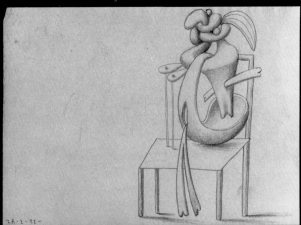

(MP 1097)

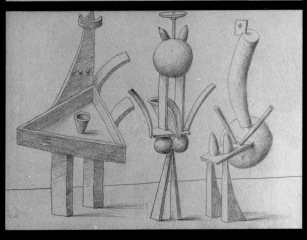

◀ *Une anatomie: trois femmes /*
An anatomy study: three women
Paris, 1 March 1933, pencil on paper, 19.5 x 27.3 cm (MP 1097)

In this drawing of three standing figures, Picasso has created emblems which give a telling account of his view of women. The figure on the left carries a tray, bearing a cup. Small button breasts represent the gender of the figure, the head is represented by a curving band with two eyes. Like a drinks vendor in a cinema, this figure may be taken to represent service. The central figure has a heavily stylised vulva, buttocks represented as two balls, and breasts projected upwards towards a plate head. This figure can be held to represent woman as the receptacle for male sexual activity. The woman on the right is even more inverted and distorted in terms of the identity assigned to her by the artist.

▼ *Une anatomie: trois femmes /*
An anatomy study: three women
Paris, 1 March 1933, pencil on paper, 19.7 x 27.1 cm (MP 1098)

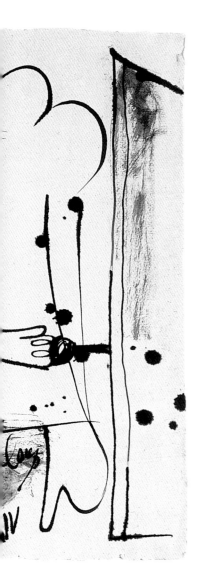

Picasso was adopted by André Breton early on as a leading member of the Surrealist movement. For a time, this suited Picasso, although he was to soon move on to a revived Classicism. His *Les demoiselles d'Avignon*, painted in 1907, was first reproduced in 1925 in the Surrealist magazine *Révolution Surréaliste*, while at the first Surrealist group exhibition that year, Picasso showed a number of Cubist compositions. The figures of three women depicted here are reduced to elemental parts or components. The cartoon quality of the drawing suggests some attempt at humour on the part of the artist, particularly with the left-hand figure. Her head has been reduced to a monocular cup, her breasts to small buttons, and from her shoulder are suspended two balls (the artist's, no doubt) – a crude and self-serving emblem of Picasso's sense of enslavement by the women in his life.

◀ Le meurtre / The murder

Boisgeloup, 10 July 1934, ink on paper, 34 x 51 cm (MP 1134)

This scene of a violent attack by a woman on a man was probably inspired by episodes in Picasso's private life. The assailant is depicted as a grotesque woman, transformed by anger into a monster, teeth bared, hair askew. In her right hand she holds a large dagger or kitchen knife, which she is about to plunge into the chest of the giant-headed man on the left, presumably a representation of Picasso himself. In this drawing, when compared with MP 1135 [not illustrated], there is more emphasis on the rage, on the action of stabbing. Both drawings were inspired by Jacques-Louis David's *The Death of Marat*.* Throughout his life, Picasso was adept at manipulating people and situations so as to depict himself in the role of victim. However, the pattern of premature deaths and suicides of several of his partners through his life perhaps tell a different story.

* This drawing was included in the exhibition at the Louvre, Paris, in 2000; *Posséder et détruire: stratégies sexuelles dans l'art d'Occident*, Michel Régis (Éditions de la Réunion des Musées Nationaux, Paris, 2000)

Bibliography

Susan Grace Galassi, 'Picasso in the Studio of Velasquez', in Jonathan Brown (ed), *Picasso and the Spanish Tradition* (Yale University Press, New Haven, 1996)

Fernande Olivier, *Loving Picasso: The Private Journal of Fernande Olivier*, Marilyn McCully (ed), (Harry N Abrams, New York, 2001)

Roland Penrose, *Picasso* (Phaidon, London, 1991)

Michel Régis, *Posséder et détruire: stratégies sexuelles dans l'art d'Occident* (Éditions de la Réunion des Musées Nationaux, Paris, 2000)

John Richardson, 'The End of the Story' in Fernande Olivier, *Loving Picasso: The Private Journal of Fernande Olivier*, Marilyn McCully (ed), (Harry N Abrams, New York, 2001)

— A *Life of Picasso, volume i*, 1881-1906 (Cape, London, 1991)

— A *Life of Picasso, volume ii*, 1907-1917 (Cape, London, 1991)

Robert Rosenblum, 'The Spanishness of Picasso's Still Lifes', in Jonathan Brown (ed), *Picasso and the Spanish Tradition* (Yale University Press, New Haven, 1995)

William Rubin and Dominique Bozo, *Pablo Picasso: A Retrospective* (Museum of Modern Art, New York, 1980)

Hélène Seckel-Klein, *Picasso und seine Sammlung* (Kunsthalle de Hypo-Kulturstiftung, 1998)

Featured Works

32 *   Portrait-charge de Paul Fort / Portrait of Paul Fort   1905
          (MP 1986-42)

34   Feuille d'études: arlequins et portraits-charge de Guillaume Apollinaire
          et d'Henri Delormel / Page of sketches: harlequins and portraits of
          Guillaume Apollinaire and of Henri Delormel   1905 (MP 509)

34-35 *   Fernande à la mantille blanche / Fernande wearing a white mantilla
          1906 (MP 510)

36-37 *   Etudes pour autoportraits / Studies for self-portraits   1906 (MP 524r)

          Etudes pour 'Les demoiselles d'Avignon': nu debout / Studies for
          'Les demoiselles d'Avignon': standing nude
37 *   1907 (MP 537)
37   1907 (MP 535, MP 536)

38   Nature morte: poisson, crâne et encrier / Still life: fish, skull and inkpot
          1908 (MP 548)

          Etudes pour 'Nu debout' / Studies for 'Standing nude'
38-39 *   1908 (MP 562)
40-41   1908 (MP 568, MP 567, MP 565, MP 564, MP 569)
41-42 *   1908 (MP 570)
43   1908 (MP 571)

43, 45 *   Nu assis / Seated nude   1908 (MP 572)

43-44 *   Etude de nu au visage hiératique, les bras croisés au-dessus de la tête /
          Study of a nude of hieratic appearance, with arms crossed above the
          head   1908 (MP 551)

44, 46 *   Etude de nu au visage hiératique, les bras croisés au-dessus de la tête /
          Study of a nude of hieratic appearance, with arms crossed above the
          head   1908 (MP 552)

46 *   Arlequin et sa compagne sur un banc / Harlequin and his companion
          on a bench   1908-09 (MP 617)

47-48 *   Femme nue debout / Nude woman standing   1908-09 (MP 631)

48   Nu assis / Seated nude   1908-09 (MP 630)

          Etudes pour 'Tête de femme (Fernande)' / Studies for 'Head of a
          woman (Fernande)'
48-49 *   1909 (MP 642)
50-51 *   1909 (MP 641)

50, 52-53 * L'homme à la moustache et à la tenora / Moustachioed man with a
          tenora   1911 (MP 659)

          Etudes pour 'Femme en chemise dans un fauteuil' / Studies for
          'Woman in a shift in an armchair'
52, 54   1913 (MP 766)
54-55 *   1913 (MP 767)

* = illustrated   MP = Musée Picasso

PICASSO – WATERCOLOURS & DRAWINGS 1896-1934

Published to coincide with the exhibition of the same name at the
Crawford Municipal Art Gallery from 13 September to 27 October 2001.

Editor   Peter Murray

© compilation copyright Crawford Municipal Art Gallery, Cork, 2001
© illustrations copyright Succession Picasso, 2001
© photographs copyright Réunion des Musées Nationaux, 2001
    (Arnaudet, Michèle Bellot, Gérard Blot, B Hatala, Hervé Lewandowski)

ISBN 0946846 766

Design   John O'Regan (© Gandon Editions, 2001)
Production   Nicola Dearey
                Sheila Holland
                produced by Gandon Editions, Kinsale
Printing   Nicholson & Bass, Belfast
Distribution   Gandon

GANDON EDITIONS
Oysterhaven, Kinsale, Co Cork, Ireland

tel   +353 (0)21-4770830
fax   +353 (0)21-4770755
e-mail   gandon@eircom.net
web-sites   www.gandon-editions.com / www.art-eire.com

CRAWFORD MUNICIPAL ART GALLERY
Emmet Place, Cork, Ireland

tel   +353 (0)21-4273377
fax   +353 (0)21-4805043
e-mail   crawfordgallery@eircom.net
web-site   www.synergy.ie/crawford

cover   *Etude de costume: le mage / Costume study: the magician*   *c.*1920

back cover   *Le meurtre / The murder*   1934

frontispiece   *Le peintre et son modèle / The painter and his model*   1930